The
Comforter

Print information available on the last page.

Rev. date: 03/16/2015

To order additional copies of this book, contact:
Xlibris
1-888-795-4274
www.Xlibris.com
Orders@Xlibris.com

Dedication

A mis querido Padres (Papi y Mami)
Para su enseñanza, todos sus
Oraciones, su gran amor, y
Su constante vigilancia en la familia.
Juan y Francisca Moyet
To my dear parents (Papi and Mami)
For their teaching, all their
Prayers, their great love, and
Their constant vigilance in the family.

John 16:33

    I have told you all this so that you may have peace in me. Here on earth you will have many trials and sorrows, but take heart, because I have overcome the world.

You are My God, and Savior, My Redeemer.

My Forever Friend, always with me, at my

Side, to guide me by The Holy Spirit that

Is within me. Ever giving of your Grace,

Mercy, and Love. How I want to always

Know you, know your peace, and always feel

Your Blessed Assurance and know that you

Are mine. Thank You Lord for all that

You have given to me.

With Love,

Your Servant

Hebrews 6:19
    We have this hope as an anchor for the soul, firm and secure.

You go before me Lord, I am not afraid,
I will follow you. Your will be done, I want
to accept it. You My Lord are The
Omnipotent. You are My Lord and My God.
All shall work out for The Good and Glory
Of God. I Love You.

Amen

John 14:27
    My peace I give unto you, let not your heart be troubled, neither let it be afraid.

You, O Lord are My Provider in all

ways and in all times. I must forever keep

in mind that my provisions come from you.

That in Your Word you've

Already promised that I would find when

I seek, should I knock The Door will

be opened, and in asking I would surely

receive. Father God I claim all your

promises. Not only this night, but every night

And Day of my life. I Thank You Jesus

For All Things.

Psalms 46:1
"God is our refuge and strength, a very present help in trouble."

Through the storm and within it,

You are there. The hand of The Almighty.

Hold on and He will take you safely to shore.

Death, Stroke, Disease whatever the storm may be.

Jesus will be with you.

Psalms 94:19
    When my anxious thoughts multiply within me, Your consolations delight my soul.

Dear Jesus,

Thank you for The Storm, for without

It I would not be able to experience

The colors of The Rainbow, that precious

Bow in the sky. I want to learn what

you are teaching me, I want to be

closer to you, and be more like you.

Everyday I will seek you, call on you,

listen so that I may here when You

Speak. I forever want to be in your will,

Be guided by The Holy Spirit and Always

Be next to you.

Love,

Me

Psalms 16:5
    O Lord, You are the portion of my inheritance and my cup; You maintain my lot.

Hello Lord,

Good Morning, All Honor be to

Your Holy Name. Thank you for another

day. May I Glorify You in all that

I do, and Praise You, Every Hour. Be with

All the children Lord, Bless this day

and them. Help them.

Amen

Psalms 63:8
My soul clings to you: your right hand upholds me.

To always be with Jesus, to never

Let go. If I had not gone through

The Storm I would not have witnessed

Your power, your grace, your mercy, your glory,

The Everything you could be in My Life if

Only I let you Lead. I tell you I want

You to Lead and I will follow, yet my

Actions show me in front of you. Yes, Lord

I know I can't see you if I'm in

Front, I then look back and I stumble.

Yet again You catch me and once again

take The Lead. I, My Lord, am ever Grateful.

Love.

Me

Jeremiah 29:11

    For I know The Plans I Have For You, Declares The Lord, Plans To Prosper You And Not To Harm You, Plans To Give You Hope And A Future.

If it were not for love shown me I dread to think where I would be. If

It were not for the kind words you speak to me. I would be like a

world in which the sun never rose.

Oh, Father God, all the important things in our life do

we see you or have we simply blocked Jesus out like

the clouds do the sun.

To where is my bow directed and to whom

Shall I bow, if both are not to Jesus,

my vessel will be tossed about.

For my only anchor could be Christ Jesus.

In all my times that I cry out, for only Jesus is

My Blessed assurance and whom I adore. Thank You

Lord for another sunset, yet another kiss goodnight.

I will make the stars my blanket and I will thank You

For my sleep tonight, and praise you for your

Goodness brought on me today, for You

Alone are worthy day after day.

Romans 14:17
    For the kingdom of God is not a matter of eating and drinking, but of righteousness, peace and joy in the Holy Spirit.

Deuteronomy 32:3
I will proclaim the name of the Lord. Oh, praise the greatness of our God!

Isaiah 26:3
        You will keep in perfect peace those whose minds are steadfast, because they trust
in you.

Romans 15:4

    "For whatever things were written before were written for our learning, that we through the patience and comfort of the scriptures might have hope."

2 Corinthians 13:14
    May the grace of the Lord Jesus Christ, and the love of God, and the fellowship of the Holy Spirit be with you all.